DISTORTED IMAGES OF SELF

RESTORING OUR VISION

DALE &
JUANITA
RYAN

8 STUDIES
FOR INDIVIDUALS
OR GROUPS

T0349961

INTER-VARSITY PRESS
36 Causton Street, London SW1P 4ST, England
Email: ivp@ivpbooks.com
Website: www.ivpbooks.com

Originally published in the United States of America in the LifeGuide® Bible Studies series in 2013 by InterVarsity Press, Downers Grove, Illinois
First published in Great Britain by Scripture Union in 2014
This edition published in Great Britain by Inter-Varsity Press 2019

British Library Cataloguing-in-Publication Data
A catalogue record for this book is available from the British Library.

ISBN: 978-1-78359-838-0

Printed in Great Britain by Ashford Colour Ltd, Gosport, Hampshire

Inter-Varsity Press publishes Christian books that are true to the Bible and that communicate the gospel, develop discipleship and strengthen the church for its mission in the world.

IVP originated within the Inter-Varsity Fellowship, now the Universities and Colleges Christian Fellowship, a student movement connecting Christian Unions in universities and colleges throughout Great Britain, and a member movement of the International Fellowship of Evangelical Students. Website: www.uccf.org.uk. That historic association is maintained, and all senior IVP staff and committee members subscribe to the UCCF Basis of Faith.

Contents

Getting the Most Out of
Distorted Images of Self

The way we think and feel about ourselves is one of the most important things about us. Our self-images have an enormous impact on our lives. Among other things, our sense of self affects our peace of mind, our creativity and our ability to engage meaningfully in the world. Perhaps most important, it affects our relationships with others, including our relationship with God.

Self-image is not a simple thing. Our ideas about ourselves tend to be complex and even conflicting, to the point that it is not uncommon for us to present one version of ourselves to the outside world and struggle with another version in private.

Our self-images tend to be constructed from our complicated emotional and relational histories. All of our relationships and experiences throughout our lives are woven into our self-concept, but our most foundational self-images, both positive and negative, take root in early life.

As children we come to conclusions about ourselves based on the mosaic of experiences we have with others. These conclusions are not logical, rational deductions. They are more like impressions of ourselves in the context of life events and interactions with others. They are interpretations made at a time when we had a very limited maturity or understanding. As a result, some of the most foundational aspects of our self-image are constructed from our limited childhood perspectives.

Unfortunately, many of us have experiences in early life that lead us to see ourselves in negative ways. These conclusions can develop into ongoing distortions in our sense of self.

Because we do not simply outgrow our distorted images of self, and because these distortions tend to be hidden from others and often from ourselves, these components of our self-image are capable of having a significant impact on what we do and think in all aspects of our lives. They can form a kind of grid through which we see ourselves well into our adulthood and potentially all the days of our lives.

Our distorted self-images are based in deep-seated fears. These fears are almost always too uncomfortable or too painful to expose to other people and often too uncomfortable or too painful to stay fully aware of ourselves. For that reason we develop ways to protect ourselves from our fears. If, for example, we live with a distorted self-image that we are unlovable, we may drive ourselves to the point of exhaustion to earn the love we fear can never be ours. Similarly, if we see ourselves as worthless, we might either do all we can to prove to others that we are valuable, or we might despair of being valued and settle for depressed, secluded lives.

Probably the most important thing to emphasize about distorted self-images is that they are not really who we are. Under all of our pretense and defensiveness, and deeper than our worst fears and distortions about ourselves, is a self that God created in God's own image. We are God's children, loved beyond our wildest imaginings, valued beyond telling, made to live in joyful reliance on our Maker, freely forgiven, fully repairable, always remembered and seen, significant in our capacity to be part of God's presence in this world, and made to live in loving community with others.

The purpose of this LifeBuilder is to help you see yourself through God's eyes of love. Thomas Merton once described the important healing work we have to do in order to live in the truth of who we really are: "We must cast off our false, exterior self like the cheap and showy garment that it is. We must find our real self in its very great and very simple dignity: created to be a child of God, and capable of loving with something of God's own sincerity."*

Because our distorted images of self are often rooted in painful emotional experiences, identifying them and pursuing healing can be an emotionally challenging experience. If you find this to be the case, we encourage you to seek out the support of a trusted friend, pastor, spiritual director or counselor. It is also important to remember that healing deeply from distorted images of self will likely mean healing slowly. None of us can change our distorted images of self simply by an act of our will or by our own effort. What we can do is invite God to heal us and seek the support we need in the process. Our prayer is that these studies will be used by the Spirit to encourage you on your journey of identifying some of your distorted images of self and in gradually displacing these distortions with biblically accurate images of yourself.

As you study these texts it is our prayer that you will learn to think and feel about yourself in ways that are consistent with the ways God thinks and feels about you. Our prayer is that you will hear God saying to you: "I love you. I value you. You are my very own, dearly loved child. This is who you are."

May your vision or who you are be renewed as you come to see yourself through God's eyes of love.

Suggestions for Individual Study

1. As you begin each study, pray that God will speak to you through his Word.

2. Read the introduction to the study and respond to the personal reflection question or exercise. This is designed to help

---

*Thomas Merton, *No Man Is an Island* (San Diego: Harcourt Brace Jovanovich, 1955).

you focus on God and on the theme of the study.

3. Each study deals with a particular passage so that you can delve into the author's meaning in that context. Read and reread the passage to be studied. The questions are written using the language of the New International Version, so you may wish to use that version of the Bible. The New Revised Standard Version is also recommended.

4. This is an inductive Bible study, designed to help you discover for yourself what Scripture is saying. The study includes three types of questions. Observation questions ask about the basic facts: who, what, when, where and how. Interpretation questions delve into the meaning of the passage. Application questions help you discover the implications of the text for growing in Christ. These three keys unlock the treasures of Scripture.

Write your answers to the questions in the spaces provided or in a personal journal. Writing can bring clarity and deeper understanding of yourself and of God's Word.

5. It might be good to have a Bible dictionary handy. Use it to look up any unfamiliar words, names or places.

6. Use the prayer suggestion to guide you in thanking God for what you have learned and to pray about the applications that have come to mind.

7. You may want to go on to the suggestion under "Now or Later," or you may want to use that idea for your next study.

Suggestions for Members of a Group Study

1. Come to the study prepared. Follow the suggestions for individual study mentioned above. You will find that careful preparation will greatly enrich your time spent in group discussion.

2. Be willing to participate in the discussion. The leader of your group will not be lecturing. Instead, he or she will be encouraging the members of the group to discuss what they have learned. The leader will be asking the questions that are found in this guide.

3. Stick to the topic being discussed. Your answers should be based on the verses which are the focus of the discussion and not on outside authorities such as commentaries or speakers. These studies focus on a particular passage of Scripture. Only rarely should you refer to other portions of the Bible. This allows for everyone to participate in in-depth study on equal ground.

4. Be sensitive to the other members of the group. Listen attentively when they describe what they have learned. You may be surprised by their insights! Each question assumes a variety of answers. Many questions do not have "right" answers, particularly questions that aim at meaning or application. Instead the questions push us to explore the passage more thoroughly.

When possible, link what you say to the comments of others. Also, be affirming whenever you can. This will encourage some of the more hesitant members of the group to participate.

5. Be careful not to dominate the discussion. We are sometimes so eager to express our thoughts that we leave too little opportunity for others to respond. By all means participate! But allow others to also.

6. Expect God to teach you through the passage being discussed and through the other members of the group. Pray that you will have an enjoyable and profitable time together, but also that as a result of the study you will find ways that you can take action individually and/or as a group.

7. Remember that anything said in the group is considered confidential and should not be discussed outside the group unless specific permission is given to do so.

8. If you are the group leader, you will find additional suggestions at the back of the guide.

1

Unlovable
Versus Loved

Ephesians 3:14-21

We are creatures. We are created in love by God who is love. We are the much-loved children of God. Scripture teaches us that all that love is, God is toward us—patient, kind, respectful, self-giving, keeping no record of wrongs, protective, hopeful. God's love for us is a love that is steadfast and unshakable. It is a love that endures forever.

Yet we struggle to trust that this is true. We may believe that God is loving, but we may not be able to live in the joy and peace of this reality because we see ourselves as unlovable. We may have constructed a self-image that assumes that something is so wrong with us that no one who knows us fully could possibly love us. Each of us has a unique story of how these false images come to take on the force of a foundational truth in our lives. But whatever our story—and however much we believe these distortions—they are not the truth about who we are.

God, who is love, loves us. This is good news. It is powerful news—powerful enough to compete with the distorted images of ourselves which seem to exercise control over our lives. It is the good news that can set us free to be the much loved children our Creator made us to be.

GROUP DISCUSSION. What negative things have you heard other people say about themselves—things which you could tell they believed—but which you could see were not true?

PERSONAL REFLECTION. What negative things do you find yourself saying to yourself about yourself?

Write a more grace-full message to replace each of the negative things you say about yourself. (This might be difficult, but give it a try.)

The text for this study is a prayer on behalf of the people at the church in Ephesus. It is a prayer that they would come to know deeply and fully the powerful truth of God's great love for them as expressed in Christ. *Read Ephesians 3:14-21.*

---

1. This prayer is directed to God the Father. What do verses 14-15 and 20 say about God?

---

2. Make a list of all the specific requests expressed in this prayer.

---

3. What thoughts do you have about this list of requests?

4. What is your thought about what verse 20 states on the heels of making all these requests?

5. What might it mean for God to strengthen us with power through the Spirit in our inner being as a way to make us ready for Christ to dwell in our hearts?

6. What might it mean for Christ to dwell in our hearts through faith, in the context of all that is being prayed here?

7. How is the love of God in Christ described in verses 18 and 19?

8. How do these words which describe God's love affect you?

9. What might it mean to be "filled to the measure of all the fullness of God"?

---

10. Sit for a few minutes of quiet and meditate on the image found in verse 17: "And I pray that you, being rooted and established in love . . ." As you can, see yourself as a parched plant being transplanted into the soil of God's rich, vast love for you. You are parched and dying because you have believed yourself unlovable in some way. But now you are being planted in the heart of God's love. Slowly, let your roots relax, and begin to take in the nourishment available in the amazing soil of love. Drink it in. Let it strengthen you with new life, new hope, new joy. Write about your experience of meditating on this image.

---

11. What do you imagine it would be like for you to be filled with God's love?

Use the prayer in this text as the basis of a prayer for yourself to know God's love.

Now or Later

Sit with the image in question 10 for a few minutes each day this week. Continue to write about your experience of letting your roots sink deeply into the soil of God's rich, vast love.

2

Worthless
Versus Valued

We are treasured by God. We are held in high esteem by our Maker. The sweeping narrative of Scripture is that God made us in God's image and seeks to live in close relationship with us. Scripture shows us a God who freely gives to us, not only good gifts but also God's very self.

We came from God. We are a part of God. We are valued by God. This value is not something we earn. It is not part of an "if-then" clause—if we do this or that, then God will value us. It is a given. It is part of the structure of the universe. We are valued.

Yet a large number of us spend our lives chasing the hope that maybe *if* we accomplish certain things, *then* we will be valued. If we are smart enough, knowledgeable enough, good looking enough, rich enough, thin enough, spiritual enough, caring enough, giving enough, then maybe we will earn some sense of worth. We strive to earn what is already ours. We *are* valuable. We *are* valued. This gift is ours to receive with humility, wonder and joy. It is ours to live in—freeing us to abandon all competition and comparison with others who are equally valued by our Maker. Freeing us to treat all others with the same great value our Creator bestows on us.

GROUP DISCUSSION. What kinds of things might communicate to a child his or her value?

PERSONAL REFLECTION. What moments come to mind of times when you felt you were being treated by someone as having little or no value?

What moments come to mind of times when you have felt valued by someone?

The text for this study is one of a trilogy of stories that Jesus told about God, who values us highly. In one story God, represented as a father, demonstrates to both a son who left home and a son who stayed home their great value as God's much-loved children. In another story God, represented as a shepherd, goes in search of the one sheep that strayed from the group and got lost. And in this story God, represented as a woman, sweeps the floors in search of the missing silver coin. *Read Luke 15:1-2, 8-10.*

1. Who were the two primary groups in the audience when Jesus told this story?

How were they outwardly different from each other?

How might they have been similar?

---

2. What specific pictures and ideas come to mind as you read this story about God as the woman who lights a lamp and sweeps in search of the lost silver coin?

---

3. If you were going to give voice to the lost coin, what might the coin be saying to itself about its value while it is lost?

---

4. How might the image of God as the woman who sweeps have been heard by the various members of Jesus' audience?

5. How might the image of us as the lost coin have been heard by the various members of Jesus' audience at the time?

---

6. What does this story tell us about God?

---

7. How does this compare and contrast with how you see God?

---

8. What does this story tell us about how God sees us?

---

9. How does this compare and contrast with how you see yourself?

---

10. In a time of quiet, imagine yourself in this story as a valuable silver coin that has been knocked off the table and has rolled into a dark corner where you have been gathering dust and grime. You are powerless to help yourself. And you have lost your shine and all sense of your value. But the woman to whom you belong lights a lamp and picks up a broom and begins to sweep the floors in search of you because of your great value. When the woman finds you, she picks you up and gently rubs the dust and grime away until your silver shine is restored. Then she throws a party, calling all her friends to celebrate. Let yourself be held in those tender, powerful hands. Let yourself experience the party in your honor. Write about your experience.

---

11. How might knowing these truths about how God sees you and values you make a difference in your life?

Thank God for valuing you so highly. Invite God to help you live in the truth of your great value to God.

Now or Later

Use the meditation from question 10 again. Allow yourself to experience your value to God, as described by this story.

3

Self-Reliant Versus God-Reliant

Isaiah 30:15-21

We are creatures. We receive in each breath, in each beat of our hearts, the gift of life from our loving Creator. In much the same way that we are designed to be sustained and strengthened by the regular intake of oxygen, we are designed to be sustained and strengthened by the ongoing intake of God's help and guidance. We are designed to live in reliance on our Maker. It is in this reliance on God that our lives are able to become the loving, joyful, rich experience they were meant to be.

Scripture teaches us that God created us to need God's help. It also teaches us that God longs to help us. Yet, all too often, we resist these good gifts from God. We resist them in part because we live with a distorted view of ourselves as self-reliant. There are various reasons why we might be attached to this image of ourselves. Self-reliance might seem like what everyone, including God, expects of us. Self-reliance might seem *strong*, whereas reliance on God might seem *weak*. Reliance on ourselves might seem like the only way to be in charge, whereas reliance on God might seem like giving up control. For some of us the thought of trusting anyone to be there for us, including God, might seem impossible. We may have concluded early in life that we are on our own, that we need to take care of ourselves.

God calls us out of this kind of distorted self-reliance and into the truth of dependence on our loving Creator. God calls us in love to know that we are not on our own. God is eager to help us and care for us.

GROUP DISCUSSION. Think about walking with a young child in an area that has major traffic hazards. What would it be like for you if the child took off and ran ahead of you, saying he wanted to do it by himself?

PERSONAL REFLECTION. In terms of your relationship with God, think of a time when you acted like the child who runs off on his or her own. What was the experience like?

In the text for this study we hear God calling us in love to ask for the care, help and guidance we need. We hear God confronting our resistance and reminding us that God is always ready and eager to help us. *Read Isaiah 30:15-21.*

---

1. In verses 15-17, how would you contrast what the Lord is calling the people to do with what the people were doing?

---

2. In what ways do you relate to what the people were doing?

3. What does it mean in verse 17 that "a thousand will flee at the threat of one; at the threat of five you will all flee away"?

4. How do the practices mentioned in verse 15 relate to living in reliance on God rather than ourselves?

5. In your experience, what is difficult about the practices of repentance, rest, quietness and trust?

6. In your experience, what are the benefits of practicing repentance, rest, quietness and trust?

7. What do we learn about God in verses 18-21?

8. What promises are made in verses 18-21?

9. Why might it be so important that we actually ask for God's help?

---

10. To repent is to turn around, to change the direction we are headed. God calls us to give up our distortions of being self-reliant and to turn to God to experience, instead, that we are creatures made to rely on God. In a time of quiet, invite God to show you how you need to repent of your self-reliance and learn anew what it is to rely on God. Write whatever you sense God is showing you.

---

11. God's call to repentance is a call to rest, to quietness and to trust. It is a call to give up all the hard work that self-reliance requires and to "let go and let God." In a second time of quiet, let yourself rest before God as you talk honestly with God about both your fears and your longings to live in trusting reliance on God. Listen to God's voice of compassion and guidance speaking to you. Write about your experience.

Thank God for God's compassion toward you, and for God's desire to guide you and help you.

Now or Later

Continue to use the focused prayers of questions 10 and 11 throughout the week, writing about your experience.

4

Condemned
Versus Forgiven

1 John 1:5–2:11

God is a forgiving God. Scripture teaches us that God "remembers our sins no more," that God "freely pardons" and that while we are actively sinning God is actively loving us. Yet we struggle to live in this truth. We struggle with the burdens of guilt and shame. We see ourselves as condemned.

Imagine the difference it would make in our lives if we lived every day with a conscious awareness that we are fully, freely forgiven by God. Imagine for a moment what our lives would be like if shame had no power over us, if guilt did not lead us to despair and if despair did not reinforce our depressive tendencies. God's desire is that we receive the gift of forgiveness and the freedom it brings from the many burdens we carry.

The path toward the freedom of forgiveness is the path of honesty and humility. As we face the truth about the harms we have done, confess the many ways we have failed to love and make amends to those we have harmed, the darkness will pass and the true Light will shine.

GROUP DISCUSSION. How would you define and compare the terms *condemned* and *forgiven*?

PERSONAL REFLECTION. How might it affect you on a daily basis
if you feel condemned? How might it affect you on a daily basis
to know yourself fully forgiven?

The text for this study confronts our denial about our hurtful,
destructive, self-serving ways and calls us to acknowledge the
truth of our sin. It reassures us of God's forgiveness and in-
structs us to take ongoing inventory of our failure to love, even
as it calls us to live more and more fully in the light and love of
God. *Read 1 John 1:5–2:11.*

---

1. This text begins by presenting us with a contrast between
lying to ourselves about the sin in our lives and telling the truth
about our sin. In your own words, how would you summarize
what is being said here?

---

2. List all the reasons you can think of why we might lie to ourselves, to others and to God about the sin in our lives.

---

3. List all the reasons you can think of—including those given
in the text—for telling the truth about the sin in our lives.

4. According to this text, what is the relationship between sin and failure to love?

---

5. How does this understanding of sin compare with your thoughts about sin?

---

6. What does it mean to hate someone?

What does it mean to love someone?

---

7. According to this text, what does hate do to us?

8. First John 2:8 talks about a process of change that is going on in us. What is it that John suggests is happening in us?

What do you think this means in practical terms?

---

9. The text promises us the gift of forgiveness and teaches us that the way to experience God's forgiveness is through honest confession to God. What would it be like to live in the grace of God's full and free forgiveness?

---

10. In a time of quiet, reflect on God as a God who freely, fully forgives. Let yourself reflect on the light of God as not condemning us but as healing and freeing us to love like God loves. See yourself sitting in the healing, loving presence of this light. As you bask in the light of God's love for you, ask God to show you where you are failing to love in your life. Write whatever comes to mind.

11. Acknowledge your failures to love in a time of confession to God. Receive the gift of God's full forgiveness, offered freely to you. Focus on the image of the darkness of hate (resentment, judgment of others, withholding of love) passing from you and the light of God's love filling you. Write whatever came to your mind as you prayed.

Thank God for the gift of forgiveness.

Now or Later

Use questions 10 and 11 in a time of prayer each day this week. Write about your experience of doing this.

5

Irreparable Versus Repairable

God is our Healer and our Help. Scripture teaches us that God is able to rescue us, restore us, transform us and make us new. God is able to replace our fear with peace and joy. God is able to remove our hearts of stone and give us hearts of flesh. God is able to heal our shame and guilt and to set us free to know ourselves as loved and valued.

This is all very good news. It is especially good news for those of us who see ourselves as damaged beyond repair. It is good news for those of us who fear that we are beyond help, including God's help.

We may put a lot of energy into hiding our sense of irreparability. We may try to cover up our fears about ourselves with attempts to look good. But the distortion of ourselves as irreparable lingers and drives us to work harder and harder while our fears increase more and more.

As we have seen in the previous studies, Scripture reminds us that we are loved, we are valued, we are not on our own, we are forgiven. In this study we are reminded that God is powerful, loving, eager and able to repair and heal us.

GROUP DISCUSSION. What might it be like to feel hopeless about being able to change for the better as a person?

PERSONAL REFLECTION. In what ways do you feel that you are beyond help or repair?

In the text for this study, we hear the story of a man who believed himself to be beyond hope, who called out to God for help and experienced restoration. *Read Psalm 30.*

---

1. How does the writer of this psalm describe himself before he experienced God's rescue and help (vv. 1, 3, 5, 7, 11)?

---

2. In what way do these descriptions match experiences you have had?

---

3. What did the writer do when he was in this desperate, hopeless situation?

4. What language does the writer use to describe what God did for him?

5. How might these descriptions of God's help speak to someone who fears that they are irreparable?

6. Which of these descriptions of God's active help speak to you the most?

7. In verse 5 the writer states that God's "anger lasts only a moment, but his favor lasts a lifetime." In verse 7 the psalmist talks to God about a time when God "hid his face." What do you think he is saying in these two statements?

8. In what way do you relate to the experiences described in verses 5 and 7?

9. How would you describe the psalmist's response to being rescued, helped and healed by God?

---

10. In a time of quiet, talk to God about your own need and distress. Talk to God about whatever feelings of fear, shame, despair or hopelessness you have about yourself. Invite God to help you and heal you. Write about what you shared with God.

---

11. God is powerful and loving and actively working to heal us. As this psalmist puts it, God is working "to turn our wailing into dancing, to remove our sackcloth and clothe us with joy." In a time of quiet, invite God to show you how God is doing this in your life. Write about whatever you sensed in this time. Stay open to whatever God might continue to show you.

Thank God for being powerful and eager to rescue, heal and restore you.

Now or Later

Continue to use questions 10 and 11 in a time of quiet with God each day this week.

6

Forgotten Versus Remembered

Genesis 16

God is frequently described in Scripture as faithful in love and goodness. God's love never fails. God's lovingkindness endures forever. God actively loves and cares for all that God has made.

We read that God's love is too vast for us to comprehend, that it surpasses our knowing. Yet we also read that it is a love that is deeply personal. Our Creator knows when every sparrow falls and knows us so intimately that even the hairs of our head are counted. God knows when we rise and when we rest, what we think and what we say.

We are known. We are seen. We are valued. We are loved. In ways that are constant, sure and everlasting. Yet some of us experience ourselves as invisible, forgotten, neglected and abandoned. These distorted images of ourselves feed our fears and loneliness.

God invites us to see and experience ourselves as seen and known. God never forgets us. In a text in Isaiah, God asks if a mother can forget her child, and goes on to say that even if a mother could forget her own child, God can never forget us. We came from God. We are God's own creation. God will never forget us.

GROUP DISCUSSION. What might it be like to feel invisible or easily forgettable to others and to God?

PERSONAL REFLECTION. Have you had times when you felt like God has forgotten you? What was the experience like?

In the text for this study we read a story about a woman who was a servant. She was a handmaiden to Sarah, wife of Abraham. She had little voice or choice in her world. She was someone who might have seemed invisible, forgettable to others. But she was seen and remembered by God. *Read Genesis 16.*

---

1. This chapter reads a bit like a four-act play (vv. 1-4, vv. 5-6, vv. 7-14, vv. 15-16). What titles might you give to each act?

---

2. What sense do you get from this story about how Sarah (Sarai) saw Hagar?

---

3. What sense do you get from this story about how Abraham saw Hagar?

4. How does Sarah's and Abraham's treatment of Hagar compare with the way God treats Hagar?

---

5. How does Hagar respond to God?

---

6. What do you imagine it was like to be Hagar—to have no voice or no choice in life and to be seen as someone's property?

---

7. Are there ways in which you relate to Hagar's experience of being treated as "less than"?

---

8. How do you relate to the experience of feeling forgotten by others, to the experience of feeling alone?

9. What would it be like to know that God does not forget you but rather remembers you and sees you with compassion?

---

10. Take a few minutes to breathe deeply and easily. Picture yourself out in the desert, having run out of supplies, crying and listening to your child cry. You have been mistreated. You believe you are forgotten and alone. But then you hear an angel of God speaking to you, telling you that you are remembered, you are seen, your misery is known to God and your needs are being provided for. Stay with the experience of being seen and remembered by God in such loving ways. Write about your experience.

---

11. What would you like to do to acknowledge and respond to the God who sees you and remembers you?

Thank God for never forgetting you.

Now or Later

Use question 10 as a prayer meditation each day this week. Write about your experience of being seen and remembered by God.

7

Insignificant Versus Significant

Matthew 5:1-10, 14-16

Who am I? we wonder. What significance does my small life have in the big world, in this vast universe? What is the point of my existence? What is the meaning of my life?

The psalmist reflected on this ancient question when he queried the Lord:

> When I consider your heavens,
>   the work of your fingers,
> the moon and the stars,
>   which you have set in place,
> what is mankind that you are mindful of them,
>   human beings that you care for them? (Psalm 8:3-4)

It is true that in many ways we are very small. We are each just one out of many billions of humans on this earth, living on a spinning sphere that is one of many billions of spheres spinning in God's great universe. But small is not the same as insignificant to our Maker. The psalmist goes on to say, quite astonishingly, about humankind that God has "crowned them with glory and honor" (v. 5).

We are crowned by God with glory. We are crowned by our Creator with honor. Yet we struggle with painful feelings of insignificance that can either drive us into desperate, exhausting efforts to "be somebody" or drive us into the despair of apathy and depression. As this text suggests, the solution is to recognize that our significance is a gift from God. It is a gift to be received with childlike humility.

GROUP DISCUSSION. What kinds of things would you say that people in our culture do in order to gain a sense of significance?

What impact do these attempts to gain significance have on peoples' character and relationships?

PERSONAL REFLECTION. What thoughts and feelings have you experienced as you reflect on your sense of significance or insignificance?

In the text for this study Jesus turns common wisdom on its head. Jesus teaches us that we do not become significant when we strive to gain power or status. All our attempts to grasp self-made glory only hide our true significance. Instead, our true significance is seen only when we abandon such attempts and allow the true glory God has given us to shine through. *Read Matthew 5:1-10, 14-16.*

---

1. Make a list of the ways of being that Jesus blesses in verses 2-10.

2. What do these characteristics have in common?

3. How does this list contrast with the list our culture sees as blessed?

4. Rewrite the list from question 1 using your own words and phrases to capture the meaning you see in each way of being.

5. Which of these character qualities challenge you or speak to you the most?

6. Look at who Jesus says we are in verse 14. Sit with this statement for a minute. Read it again. What thoughts do you have about being told that this is who you are?

7. What does Jesus say in verses 14-16 about the ways people might respond to the reality of their God-given significance?

8. Why would we hide our true significance?

9. What is it about the character qualities that Jesus blessed in verses 2-10 that allows our lights to shine in a way that would "give light to everyone in the house"?

10. In a time of quiet, see yourself as a lamp lit but hidden. Ask God to show you what is blocking God's light of love from shining. Invite God to remove, bit by bit, the things which conceal your light. Write about your experience.

11. In a time of quiet, see yourself as a light lit and sitting on a stand, providing light for others. Write about your experience of being the light that you are.

Thank God for the gift of significance.

Now or Later

Use questions 6, 10 and 11 in a time of reflection and prayer this week. Write about your experience.

8

Disconnected Versus Bonded in Love

1 John 4:7-21

We are all created with a need to be deeply bonded to others and to our Maker. We are designed to belong to someone greater than ourselves and to each other. This is the core of who we are.

Yet we often feel like the odd person out. We often see ourselves as disconnected, different and alone. And when we see ourselves in this way, we are usually unaware that many others around us are feeling the same way. Single, married, with or without children, young or old, rich or poor, this view of ourselves as outsiders can affect any of us.

But this way of seeing ourselves is a distortion. We do belong. We are loved. Whether we know it or experience it, this is the truth about us. We belong. We are connected to God and to others.

In the text for this study we are reminded that we live in relationship with our Creator and in relationship with each other.

GROUP DISCUSSION. What does belonging mean to you?

PERSONAL REFLECTION. What is it like to feel disconnected from others and from God?

What helps you to feel connected to God and to others?

In the text for this study we read that God is love, that God loves us first and always and calls us to experience the richness that comes from knowing ourselves to be deeply bonded in love to God and to each other. *Read 1 John 4:7-21.*

1. List several things we learn about God in this text.

2. What are the effects of knowing God, according to this text?

3. How does this kind of knowing differ from an academic knowing of God?

4. What does the text say about how God showed love to us (vv. 9-10)?

5. Given this gift of love from God, what might it mean, in practical terms, to love each other?

---

6. The text seems to be talking about a progression of love between God, ourselves and others. Why might it be important to know that this progression of love begins with God—to know that God loved us first?

---

7. In verse 16 we read that "we know and rely on the love God has for us." What would it be like to know and rely on God's love for you?

---

8. According to verse 18, fear and love seem to be in opposition to each other. Fear causes us to feel disconnected and alone in the world. How does fear create barriers to knowing and relying on the love of God?

---

9. In what way does fear create barriers to knowing and relying on other peoples' love?

10. In what way does fear create barriers to freely loving others?

---

11. In a time of quiet, close each hand and picture the fears that create barriers to receiving love from God and from others as items held tightly in your fists. Invite God to help you release your fears to God's loving care. As you are ready, open your hands and keep them open in an act of release. Then read verse 16 three times slowly, giving yourself a couple of minutes to sit with these truths between each reading. "And so we know and rely on the love God has for us. God is love. Whoever lives in love lives in God, and God in them." As you keep your hands open, invite God to fill you with a deeper experience of God's love, freeing you to love more and more as God loves. Write about your experience of praying in this way.

Thank God that God loves us first and calls us to live in that love, and to be that love to others.

Now or Later

Continue to use question 11 in a time of daily prayer and reflection this week. Write about your experience of praying in this way. Notice any sense of feeling more deeply bonded in love to God and to others.

Leader's Notes

Leading a Bible discussion can be an enjoyable and rewarding experience. But it can also be *scary*—especially if you've never done it before. If this is your feeling, you're in good company. When God asked Moses to lead the Israelites out of Egypt, he replied, "O Lord, please send someone else to do it!" (Ex 4:13). It was the same with Solomon, Jeremiah and Timothy, but God helped these people in spite of their weaknesses, and he will help you as well.

You don't need to be an expert on the Bible or a trained teacher to lead a Bible discussion. The idea behind these inductive studies is that the leader guides group members to discover for themselves what the Bible has to say. This method of learning will allow group members to remember much more of what is said than a lecture would.

These studies are designed to be led easily. As a matter of fact, the flow of questions through the passage from observation to interpretation to application is so natural that you may feel that the studies lead themselves. This study guide is also flexible. You can use it with a variety of groups—student, professional, neighborhood or church groups. Each study takes forty-five to sixty minutes in a group setting.

There are some important facts to know about group dynamics and encouraging discussion. The suggestions listed below should enable you to effectively and enjoyably fulfill your role as leader.

Preparing for the Study

1. Ask God to help you understand and apply the passage in your own life. Unless this happens, you will not be prepared to lead others. Pray too for the various members of the group. Ask God to open your hearts to the message of his Word and motivate you to action.

2. Read the introduction to the entire guide to get an overview of the entire book and the issues which will be explored.

3. As you begin each study, read and reread the assigned Bible passage to familiarize yourself with it.

4. This study guide is based on the New International Version of the Bible. It will help you and the group if you use this translation as the basis for your study and discussion.

5. Carefully work through each question in the study. Spend time in meditation and reflection as you consider how to respond.

6. Write your thoughts and responses in the space provided in the study guide. This will help you to express your understanding of the passage clearly.

7. It might help to have a Bible dictionary handy. Use it to look up any unfamiliar words, names or places. (For additional help on how to study a passage, see chapter five of *How to Lead a LifeBuilder Study,* IVP, 2018.)

8. Consider how you can apply the Scripture to your life. Remember that the group will follow your lead in responding to the studies. They will not go any deeper than you do.

9. Once you have finished your own study of the passage, familiarize yourself with the leader's notes for the study you are leading. These are designed to help you in several ways. First, they tell you the purpose the study guide author had in mind when writing the study. Take time to think through how the study questions work together to accomplish that purpose. Second, the notes provide you with additional background information or suggestions on group dynamics for various questions. This information can be useful when people have difficulty understanding or answering a question. Third, the leader's notes can alert you to potential problems you may encounter during the study.

10. If you wish to remind yourself of anything mentioned in the leader's notes, make a note to yourself below that question in the study.

Leading the Study

1. Begin the study on time. Open with prayer, asking God to help the group to understand and apply the passage.

2. Be sure that everyone in your group has a study guide. Encourage the group to prepare beforehand for each discussion by reading the introduction to the guide and by working through the questions in the study.

3. At the beginning of your first time together, explain that these studies are meant to be discussions, not lectures. Encourage the members of the group to participate. However, do not put pressure on those who may be hesitant to speak during the first few sessions. You may want to suggest the following guidelines to your group.

☐ Stick to the topic being discussed.

☐ Your responses should be based on the verses which are the focus of the discussion and not on outside authorities such as commentaries or speakers.

☐ These studies focus on a particular passage of Scripture. Only rarely should you refer to other portions of the Bible. This allows for everyone to participate in in-depth study on equal ground.

☐ Anything said in the group is considered confidential and will not be discussed outside the group unless specific permission is given to do so.

☐ We will listen attentively to each other and provide time for each person present to talk.

☐ We will pray for each other.

4. Have a group member read the introduction at the beginning of the discussion.

5. Every session begins with a group discussion question. The question or activity is meant to be used before the passage is read. The question introduces the theme of the study and encourages group members to begin to open up. Encourage as many members as possible to participate, and be ready to get the discussion going with your own response.

This section is designed to reveal where our thoughts or feelings need to be transformed by Scripture. That is why it is especially important not to read the passage before the discussion question is asked. The passage will tend to color the honest reactions people would otherwise give because they are, of course, supposed to think the way the Bible does.

You may want to supplement the group discussion question with an icebreaker to help people to get comfortable. See the community section of the *Small Group Starter Kit* (IVP, 1995) for more ideas.

You also might want to use the personal reflection question with your group. Either allow a time of silence for people to respond individually or discuss it together.

6. Have a group member (or members if the passage is long) read aloud the passage to be studied. Then give people several minutes to read the passage again silently so that they can take it all in.

7. Question 1 will generally be an overview question designed to briefly survey the passage. Encourage the group to look at the whole passage, but try to avoid getting sidetracked by questions or issues that will be addressed later in the study.

8. As you ask the questions, keep in mind that they are designed to be used just as they are written. You may simply read them aloud. Or you may prefer to express them in your own words.

There may be times when it is appropriate to deviate from the study guide. For example, a question may have already been answered. If so, move on to the next question. Or someone may raise an important question not covered in the guide. Take time to discuss it, but try to keep the group from going off on tangents.

9. Avoid answering your own questions. If necessary, repeat or rephrase them until they are clearly understood. Or point out something you read in the leader's notes to clarify the context or meaning. An eager group quickly becomes passive and silent if they think the leader will do most of the talking.

10. Don't be afraid of silence. People may need time to think about the question before formulating their answers.

11. Don't be content with just one answer. Ask, "What do the rest of you think?" or "Anything else?" until several people have given answers to the question.

12. Acknowledge all contributions. Try to be affirming whenever possible. Never reject an answer. If it is clearly off-base, ask, "Which verse led you to that conclusion?" or again, "What do the rest of you think?"

13. Don't expect every answer to be addressed to you, even though this will probably happen at first. As group members become more at ease, they will begin to truly interact with each other. This is one sign of healthy discussion.

14. Don't be afraid of controversy. It can be very stimulating. If you don't resolve an issue completely, don't be frustrated. Move on and keep it in mind for later. A subsequent study may solve the problem.

15. Periodically summarize what the group has said about the passage. This helps to draw together the various ideas mentioned and gives continuity to the study. But don't preach.

16. At the end of the Bible discussion you may want to allow group members a time of quiet to work on an idea under "Now or Later." Then discuss what you experienced. Or you may want to encourage group members to work on these ideas between meetings. Give an opportunity during the session for people to talk about what they are learning.

17. Conclude your time together with conversational prayer, adapting the prayer suggestion at the end of the study to your group. Ask for God's help in following through on the commitments you've made.

18. End on time.

Many more suggestions and helps are found in *How to Lead a LifeBuilder Study.*

Components of Small Groups

A healthy small group should do more than study the Bible. There are four components to consider as you structure your time together.

Nurture. Small groups help us to grow in our knowledge and love of God. Bible study is the key to making this happen and is the foundation of your small group.

Community. Small groups are a great place to develop deep friendships with other Christians. Allow time for informal interaction before and after each study. Plan activities and games that will help you get to know each other. Spend time having fun together going on a picnic or cooking dinner together.

Worship and prayer. Your study will be enhanced by spending time praising God together in prayer or song. Pray for each other's needs and keep track of how God is answering prayer in your group. Ask God to help you to apply what you are learning in your study.

Outreach. Reaching out to others can be a practical way of applying what you are learning, and it will keep your group from becoming self-focused. Host a series of evangelistic discussions for your friends or neighbors. Clean up the yard of an elderly friend. Serve at a soup kitchen together, or spend a day working in the community.

Many more suggestions and helps in each of these areas are found in the *Small Group Starter Kit*. You will also find information on building a small group. Reading through the starter kit will be worth your time.

Study 1. Unlovable Versus Loved. Ephesians 3:14-21.
Purpose: To challenge the distortion that we are unlovable, and to grow in our ability to see ourselves as loved by God.

Question 1. God is described as the Father of the whole family on earth and in heaven, as one who has glorious riches, as one who has the power to do immeasurably more than we ask or imagine, and as one whose power is at work within us.

Question 2. It can be helpful to make a list of all that is being asked in this prayer because each request is in itself so significant and powerful.

Question 3. Encourage people to talk about whatever mixture of thoughts and feelings they have about this prayer and all the requests that are included in it. It can seem overwhelming, too much to hope or ask for, too good to be true. It can, at the same time, feel deeply moving because it touches the deepest longings of our hearts.

Question 4. After making several huge requests, the writer states that God is able to do more than we can ask or imagine. Just when our minds and hearts are being stretched by the requests of this prayer, the writer reminds us that there is more, always so much more to all that God can and will do in love for us.

Question 5. The prayer that God would strengthen us with power through the Spirit in our inner being is a prayer that God would make us ready to receive God's love. It echoes Old Testament texts about preparing the way for the coming of the Lord, by making the paths smooth.

Question 6. We use this language often without really talking about what it might mean. It seems evident in the context here that this is not a prayer that the people would "make a decision for Christ." Rather it seems to be about God healing us deeply so that God, who is love—Christ who is love—can fill us with the love that is God, a love so vast that it "surpasses knowledge."

Question 8. Encourage people to talk about the impact of these descriptions of the vastness of God's love.

Question 9. This is a mind-bending, heart-opening image. It is a statement that we might ordinarily read right past because it is so huge. Encourage people to sit with it and let it stretch their minds and hearts in wonder.

Question 10. Because the wounds that gave birth to our distorted images are often lodged deeply within us, healing from these distortions will require that we engage our intellects, our emotions, our wills and our imaginations. This activity is an opportunity to begin an encounter between our distorted images of self and the image of self offered in Scripture. We encourage you to ask God to be present with the members of your group in the quiet moments of meditation you provide.

Give participants a few minutes of silence. You might encourage them to sit comfortably with their feet on the floor and their hands open on their laps, and to take a few deep, easy breaths as they relax a bit. You might want to then read this image (from the text and from what follows in the question) aloud:

"And I pray that you, [will be] rooted and established in love." See yourself as a parched plant being transplanted into the soil of God's rich, vast love for you. You are parched and dying because you have believed yourself unlovable in some way. But now you are being planted in the heart of God's love. Slowly, let your roots relax, and begin to take in the nourishment available in this amazing soil of love. Drink it in. Let it strengthen you with new life, new hope, new joy.

Then let the group sit quietly for a few minutes. Provide a few minutes for group members to write about their experience before you invite them to share whatever they might want to share.

Question 11. Encourage participants to imagine how their lives might change as they grow in their ability to be filled with God's love.

Study 2. Worthless Versus Valued. Luke 15:1-2, 8-10.

Purpose: To challenge the distortion that we are worthless and to grow in our ability to see ourselves as valued by God.

Question 1. The text tells us that Jesus was speaking to "tax collectors and sinners" and also to the "Pharisees and the teachers of the law." In some ways these two groups are quite different. The tax collectors and sinners represent people who may have despaired of keeping the law. They can't "get it all right," and they probably know it. The Pharisees and the teachers of the law are people who are spending their lives striving to please God by "getting it all right." They not only think they can "get it all right," they would probably tell you that they have done so!

But in spite of these differences these two groups of people have something very important in common. Both groups understand the way to God as being fundamentally about personal performance or achievement. The sinners may have given up on being good enough— they can't win in the religious performance competition. But the religious leaders who are working compulsively (even addictively) to make sure their religious performance is flawless are also playing the same game. There are no winners in this game. None of us can do enough, feel enough, believe enough, anything enough to acquire a sense of being valued by God—because our value is a gift that is already ours.

Question 2. Help participants engage more fully with this story by encouraging them to paint a verbal picture of the woman Jesus is describing. What do they imagine? A small house or shack? A woman with an apron on, with a broom in hand, sweeping, searching for this one lost coin?

Question 3. Again, help participants engage with the story by giving the image of a lost coin some thought. One striking reality about the coin is that it became lost through no fault of its own. It didn't run away or wander off. Someone else knocked it out of its place. And now it is powerless to do anything to help itself. In the other two stories of this trilogy, there is a son who returns home and a lamb who could at least bleat for help as it waits caught in the thicket. But the coin cannot do anything to assist in its own rescue. Another reality is that this coin is truly lost. It has been knocked off the dresser and rolled into some dark place where it requires diligent searching to be found. It may be covered with dust and grime. It may not look like the shiny silver coin that used to be on top of the dresser.

Question 4. The image of God as a woman who sweeps, searching for us, is a stunning one in our culture and our time. We do not talk of God in feminine terms very often, much less as a woman who is keeping house, sweeping. As surprising as this image is to us, to Jesus' original audience this must have seemed truly outrageous in many ways. Women in Jesus' time and culture were not educated, were not able to be witnesses in a court of law, were treated as property and had few rights of any kind. Only poor women, housewives, maids and servants would be found sweeping.

Question 5. The image of the lost coin certainly would have challenged the idea that if we work hard enough and are good enough, we will gain God's favor. The coin's powerlessness over its lost condition, its need for rescue, its value in God's eyes, and God's active pursuing of the coin would have spoken hope into the fear and despair which both the sinners and the religious leaders may have been privately experiencing.

Question 6. This story shows us that God loves and values us. It shows us that God values us enough to pursue us, seeking to rescue us from our lost condition. The story also shows us that God is humble. Here, God is a woman sweeping, searching in the dark corners and in the dust and grime for us. It also shows us that God has not forgotten who we are. We may be covered in dust, but God knows we are precious silver coins.

Question 7. Encourage participants to give some thought to how the image of God that Jesus presents in the story of the lost coin compares and contrasts with their own images of God.

Question 8. The story tells us that even if we feel like one of many who will never be missed, God values us individually. It tells us that God never forgets who we are. God never forgets who God created us to be. God remembers that we are shinny silver under the dust and grime. It tells us that God values us enough to come into the dark and the dirt where we have fallen. It tells us that God celebrates when we are found. The story tells us that we are so valued by God that God throws a party for us.

Question 9. Again, encourage participants to look at the contrasts between how they view themselves and how God sees them. Keep the thought in mind that our goal is to come to see ourselves in ways that are consistent with how God sees us.

Question 10. Because the wounds that gave birth to our distorted images are often lodged deep within us, healing from these distortions will require that we engage our intellects, our emotions, our wills and our imaginations. This activity is an opportunity to begin an encounter between our distorted images of self and the image of self offered in Scripture. We encourage you to ask God to meet people in the quiet moments of meditation you provide.

Provide group participants a few minutes of silence. You might encourage them to sit comfortably with their feet on the floor and their hands open on their laps, and to take a few deep, easy breaths as they relax a bit. You might want to then read this image (from the text and from what follows in the question) aloud:

See yourself in this story as a valuable silver coin that has been knocked off the table and has rolled into a dark corner where you have been gathering dust and grime. You are powerless to help yourself. And you have lost all sense of your value. But the woman to whom you belong lights a lamp, picks up a broom and begins to sweep the floors in search of you because of your great value. When the woman finds you, she picks you up and gently rubs the dust and grime away until your silver shine is restored. Then she throws a party. She calls all her friends to celebrate. Let yourself be held in those tender, powerful hands. Let yourself experience the party.

Then let the group sit quietly for a few minutes of reflection, followed by a few minutes to write about their experience before you invite them to share whatever they might want to share.

Question 11. Encourage participants to imagine the freedom, peace and joy they might experience as they grow in their ability to know themselves to be deeply valued by God.

Study 3. Self-Reliant Versus God-Reliant. Isaiah 30:15-21.

Purpose: To challenge the distortion that we are self-reliant and to grow in our ability to rely on God.

Question 1. The Lord is calling the people to rely on God's compassion, graciousness, wisdom, guidance, strength and help. But the people are refusing.

Question 2. Encourage participants to look at ways in which they "do it on their own" in their lives. Perhaps it doesn't even occur to some that they can ask for God's help and wisdom in everything. Perhaps it hasn't occurred to others that even our resistance to God's help is something we can ask God to heal.

Question 3. This is an image of hyper-reactivity and fear. A thousand people fleeing because one person is seen as a threat, or all of a city or nation fleeing because five people are seen as a threat are images of unnecessary terror. This kind of reactivity is what comes from failing to ask for God's help. We are left feeling anxious, alone, on our own, threatened and reactive.

Question 4. The description of rest and quietness is a stark contrast to the image of one thousand fleeing at the sight of one. Repentance and rest save us from our self-reliance and all the problems our self-reliance creates. *Quietness* and *trust* are words that describe what it is like to rely on God, who is our true strength.

Rest is ceasing from labor. Quietness is ceasing from talking, moving, communicating. When we repent (turn around, change our way of being) from our self-reliance and we begin to rely on (trust) God to help us, we are able to rest, we are quieted, we are able to live in peace.

Question 5. Encourage people to share honestly about the thoughts and fears that make it difficult for them to repent from self-reliance, that make it difficult to cease activity for a time and rest, that make it difficult to be quiet, and that make it difficult to trust and rely on God.

Question 7. We learn that God is gracious, compassionate, just, longing and eager to help us, waiting for us to ask for help, offering guidance.

Question 8. We are promised blessing, the end of weeping, a response to our call for help, graciousness and guidance.

Question 9. The act of asking is an acknowledgment of our need and our dependence. It is also an act of acknowledging God.

Questions 10-11. Give participants a time of quiet to pray and write as they choose. Invite them to share to the extent they feel comfortable.

Study 4. Condemned Versus Forgiven. 1 John 1:5–2:11.

Purpose: To challenge the distortion that we are condemned, and to grow in our ability to see ourselves as forgiven by God.

Question 1. These will be familiar words to some, if not most, group members. So having participants put the text into their own words provides a way to help them pay attention to what is being said more fully.

Question 2. We might lie to ourselves, to others and to God about our sin because we want to see ourselves as better than we are. We might do so out of shame, out of fear of rejection, out of avoidance of consequences.

Question 3. Telling the truth about our sin, according to the text, opens the way for us to receive God's forgiveness. It makes it possible for us to be in true relationship with others. It allows us to walk in God's light. It also frees us from hiding, from shame and from the burden of guilt. It opens the way for us to change. It allows us to live from a place of honesty, humility and courage. It helps us let go of pretense and falseness. It opens us up to God's transforming grace and power.

Question 4. Sin is characterized as "walking in the darkness," which is equivalent in this text to "hating a brother or sister." Freedom from sin is characterized as "walking in God's light," which is equivalent in this text to "loving a brother or sister" and "living as Jesus did." Sin, then, is our failure to love like Jesus loves, like God loves.

Question 5. It is not uncommon for us to think of sin as a violation of God's rules. But, as Jesus showed us and taught us, the problem is

deeper than a lack of compliance with rules. Sin is about the failure
to love. Encourage people to compare and contrast these two under-
standings of sin, and to discuss how this might affect their way of
thinking about sin.

Question 6. Encourage participants to discuss specifically and prac-
tically what these two terms—*hate* and *love*—mean in our lives and
relationships. Love is patient, kind, respectful, hopeful, merciful
and deeply values others. Hate devalues others, is full of judgment
and disrespect, and lacks mercy or kindness.

Question 7. According to this text, when we hate others, when we
fail to love others, we are in the dark, stumbling around. Our hate,
our failure to love, leaves us blind—blind to how God sees others,
blind to God's love for others and blind to who we are called to be as
followers of Jesus.

Question 8. First John 2:8 is talking about a process of healing and
transformation that God is doing in our lives. We do not love per-
fectly. We often don't love very well at all. But God's light is shining,
revealing our sin, calling us to acknowledge the truth of our failures,
offering us love and forgiveness, offering to empower us more and
more to love like Christ loves.

Question 9. Encourage participants to reflect on what the freedom of
forgiveness might mean in their lives.

Questions 10-11. Because the wounds that gave birth to our distorted images are often lodged deep within us, healing from those
distortions will require that we engage our intellects, our emotions,
our wills and our imaginations. This activity is an opportunity to
begin an encounter between our distorted images of self and the image of self offered in Scripture. We encourage you to ask God to meet
people in the quiet moments of meditation you provide.

Give participants time to work through each of these exercises
and to write about their experiences. Let them know that whatever
they experience or write is private, and they are not expected to share
unless they choose to do so. When they have worked through all
three exercises, invite them to share as they choose. They may want
to share in a general way about what it was like to spend this time in
prayer and reflection.

Study 5. Irreparable Versus Repairable. Psalm 30.

Purpose: To challenge the distortion that we are beyond repair, and to grow in our ability to see ourselves as repairable by God.

Question 1. The psalmist describes himself as being in the depths, of being in a grave, of being close to going down into a pit, of experiencing God's face turned away from him and of wailing while wearing the sackcloth that mourners wear. This is a description of great physical, emotional, mental and spiritual suffering. It is a description of feeling that one is beyond hope and beyond help.

Question 2. Encourage participants to share what they feel comfortable sharing of times when they experienced distress or suffering, especially times when they may have seen themselves as beyond help or as irreparable.

Question 3. The writer says that he called to God for help and mercy (vv. 3, 8, 10).

Question 4. The psalmist says that God lifted him, healed him, brought him up from the grave, spared him from going down into the pit, turned his wailing into dancing, and removed his sackcloth and clothed him in joy.

Question 5. The psalmist uses the language of miracle. His descriptions are all of a God who does what is seemingly impossible—a God who can repair and restore us no matter how hopeless it seems.

Question 6. Encourage participants to look at these descriptive phrases and let them speak to whatever fears they may have about being beyond God's help or capacity to repair.

Question 7. The psalmist is talking about the spiritual distress he experienced when things felt so hopeless. His perception was that even God had abandoned him and given up on him. This is a common kind of suffering when we are feeling hopeless and beyond repair. Perhaps it is the deepest kind of suffering.

Questions 10-11. Give participants time to pray, reflect and write. Invite them to share as they choose. Thank them for whatever they share with the group.

Study 6. Forgotten Versus Remembered. Genesis 16.

Purpose: To challenge the distortion that we are forgotten and to grow in our ability to see ourselves as remembered by God.

Question 1. The purpose of this question is to help participants get an overview of the drama that takes place in this text.

Question 2. Sarah seems to have seen Hagar as property. First, Sarah uses Hagar to conceive and bear a child for Abraham and herself. Second, Sarah abuses Hagar, treating her in the worst possible way—so badly that Hagar fled to the desert where she was likely to die. Sarah treated Hagar as "less than," as unimportant, as someone with very little value.

Question 3. Abraham seems passive in this story. He sleeps with Hagar at Sarah's suggestion and uses her in this way. He passively condones Sarah's abuses of Hagar. In these ways he seems to see Hagar as having little value. It seems that Hagar was almost invisible to Abraham.

Question 4. God's treatment of Hagar is a stunning contrast to how she was treated by Sarah and Abraham. God sent an angel to her who carried on a conversation with her, asking her questions, giving her guidance and promising her a son. The angel also told her that God knew what she had been suffering. God saw her, knew her, cared about her. God had not forgotten.

Question 5. Hagar responds to God's lovingkindness by giving God a new name. Hagar names God *the One who sees me.* She exclaims that she has seen the One who has seen her.

Question 6. Encourage participants to put themselves in Hagar's place as much as possible and imagine what life would be like.

Questions 7-9. Encourage participants to share as personally in response to these questions as they feel comfortable doing.

Question 10. Because the wounds that gave birth to our distorted images of ourselves are often lodged deep within us, healing from those distortions will require that we engage our intellects, our emotions, our wills and our imaginations. This activity is an opportunity to begin an encounter between our distorted images of self and the image of self offered in Scripture. We encourage you to ask God to meet people in the quiet moments of meditation you provide. You might want to read the following aloud, taking your time to do so.

Take a few minutes to breathe deeply and easily. Picture yourself out in the desert, having run out of supplies, crying and listening to your child cry. You have been mistreated. You believe yourself to be forgotten and alone. But then you hear God speaking to you, telling you that you are remembered, you are seen, your misery is known to God, and your needs are being provided. Stay with the experience of being seen and remembered by God in such loving ways. Write about your experience.

Question 11. People may want to offer words of gratitude or write a brief letter to God.

Study 7. Insignificant Versus Significant. Matthew 5:1-10, 14-16.

Purpose: To challenge the distortion that we are insignificant and to grow in our ability to see ourselves as significant to God.

Question 1. Jesus blesses those who are poor in spirit, those who mourn, those who are meek, those who hunger and thirst for righteousness, the merciful, the pure in heart, the peacemakers, and those who are persecuted for their righteousness.

Question 2. These ways of being in the world are not powerful, not seen as successful, not qualities most cultures value. They are ways of being that are humble, gentle, God-seeking, open hearted, surrendered to God and concerned with the well-being of others.

Question 3. This list is the opposite of being defended, self-seeking, power greedy, money hungry, self-righteous or closed hearted. They challenge us to open our hearts and lives to God and to each other in honesty, humility and service.

Question 4. Encourage participants to use their own words in rewriting this list to get a stronger sense of the heart of what Jesus was saying here.

Question 5. Encourage people to share which way of being speaks to them the most and why.

Question 6. "You are the light of the world." This is an astonishing statement. Sometimes the most astonishing statements are those we read past because they are hard to take in. So encourage participants to read this, reread it, sit with it, let it soak in. And then talk about it together.

Question 7. Jesus draws a contrast between two choices. We can hide our true selves, our light, under a bowl, or we can let it shine.

Question 8. This is an important question for your group to talk about because, at face value, it might not make much sense. But one reason we hide our true significance is that we don't think it is true. This is not how we see ourselves. Another reason might be that letting the light in us shine means living according to the priorities that Jesus provides in chapter 5 of Matthew's Gospel.

Question 9. The ways of being that Jesus listed are descriptions of living open-hearted, humble, loving lives. It is love that shines like a light to others. It is active love that is God's light in us.

Questions 10-11. Because the wounds that gave birth to our distorted images of ourselves are often lodged deep within us, healing from these distortions will require that we engage our intellects, our emotions, our wills and our imaginations. This activity is an opportunity to begin an encounter between our distorted images of self and the image of self offered in Scripture. We encourage you to ask God to meet group members in the quiet moments of meditation you provide. You might want to read the following aloud, taking your time to do so.

For question 10: In a time of quiet, see yourself as a lamp lit but hidden. Ask God to show you what is blocking God's light of love from shining. Invite God to remove the bowl which hides the light. Write about your experience.

For question 11: In a time of quiet, see yourself as a light lit and sitting on a stand, providing light for others. Write about your experience of being this light.

Study 8. Disconnected Versus Bonded in Love. 1 John 4:7-21.
Purpose: To challenge the distortion that we are disconnected and to grow in our ability to see ourselves as called and capable of being bonded in love to God and others.

Question 1. We learn that love comes from God. We learn that God is love. God loved us before we loved God. God showed God's love to us in Jesus' birth, life, death and resurrection. God lives in us and God's love is made complete in us.

Question 2. According to this text, if we know God, we love others. If we love others, we know God.

Question 3. This text says multiple times that to know God is to love others. This kind of "knowing God" is clearly quite different from merely knowing the facts about God. It is a very relational kind of knowing. Knowing God means loving other people. This text does not support any absolute distinction between a *vertical* relationship with God and a *horizontal* relationship with others. The two are not easily separable—they lie on the same axis. To love God is to love others. To love others is to love God.

Question 5. The love God has shown us is an active, self-giving love. Because "God lives in us and his love is made complete in us," our love will also be an active, self-giving love.

Question 6. It is important to remember that everything begins with God. Our life begins with God. Our love begins with God. It is as we come to know God's love that our hearts open to receive and then to respond in love and joy—both to God and to others. In this way we begin to move out of our sense of being disconnected and grow in the reality of our bond of love with God and others. Here is how I [Juanita] described this elsewhere:

> God is the initiator. We, the creatures, are the responders. God breathes out. We breathe in and live. God, who is with us always, calls us, longs for us, seeks fuller relationship with us. . . .
>
> We are partners in a dance. A dance in which we are clearly not in the lead. We are the responders, the receivers, and also often the resisters of these endless movements of grace. As we dance in these ways with God, and learn to resist less and less, we begin to hear the love song our Maker continually sings over us and our hearts respond with songs of love in return. Our hearts open. And gratitude pours out, and joy. We experience the truth of who we are, that we are the much loved children of God. . . . We are changing. We are being set free to know that we are loved. We are being freed to love. Breathing in the life and love that is God, breathing out the love of God to others. (Juanita Ryan, *An Enduring Embrace: Experiencing the Love at the Heart of Prayer* [Seattle: CreateSpace, 2012], pp. 5, 7.)

Question 7. Encourage participants to imagine how being able to more deeply trust God's love would change them and impact their lives.

Questions 8-10. Encourage participants to think about specific fears that create barriers to their knowing and relying on God's love, to knowing and relying on the love of others, and to their freedom to love like God loves.

Question 11. Because the wounds that gave birth to our distorted images of self are often lodged deep within us, healing from these distortions will require that we engage our intellects, our emotions, our wills and our imaginations. This activity is an opportunity to begin an encounter between our distorted images of self and the image of self offered in Scripture. We encourage you to ask God to meet members of your group in the quiet moments of meditation you provide. You might want to read the following aloud, taking your time to do so.

In a time of quiet, close each hand and picture the fears that create barriers to receiving love from God and from others as items held tightly in your fists. Invite God to help you release your fears to God's loving care. As you are ready, open your hands and keep them open in an act of release. Then read verse 16 three times slowly, giving yourself a couple of minutes to sit with these truths between each reading. "And so we know and rely on the love God has for us. God is love. Whoever lives in love lives in God, and God in them." As you keep your hands open, invite God to fill you with a deeper knowing of God's love, freeing you to know yourself as bonded to God and others in love. Write about your experience of praying in this way.

Dale Ryan is CEO of Christian Recovery International. He is also assistant professor of recovery ministry and director of the Fuller Institute of Recovery Ministry at Fuller Theological Seminary. Juanita Ryan is a clinical nurse with an M.S.N. in psychiatric mental health nursing. She is currently a therapist in private practice at Brea Family Counseling Center in Brea, California. Juanita is also the author of the LifeBuilder Bible Studies Waiting for God, The 23rd Psalm *and* Praying the Psalms. *Together Dale and Juanita authored* Distorted Images of God.